Progressive Pieces
for Clawhammer Banjo

Transcribed and arranged from
Frank Converse's *Analytical Banjo Method* (1887)

BY

JOSEPH WEIDLICH

ISBN 978-1-57424-349-9

Table of Contents

Introduction

The revised and enlarged edition of Frank Converse's *Analytical Banjo Method* (1887) contains a number of "Progressive Pieces" in the *Banjo Style*, i.e., what today we call clawhammer banjo style. These 34 pieces can perhaps be considered the pinnacle of "Banjo Style" in terms of the fluid and intricate technique required to play them with apparent ease. In addition, Converse included five additional pieces in banjo style in his section on Miscellaneous Pieces (**I have indicated these selections with an asterisk in the Song List**).

All of the pieces found in this method were written in staff notation, thus I have had to transcribe and arrange them for clawhammer banjo style in "user friendly" banjo tab. One particular quirk is that many phrases are based on thumb-lead style, i.e., notes on the beat are often played with the thumb with the index finger playing notes on the off-beat vs. the usual index-thumb right hand sequence used in contemporary clawhammer banjo practice. Let's compare the opening phrase of *Old Virginny Dance* (**x** stands for the thumb, while **1** is for the index finger):

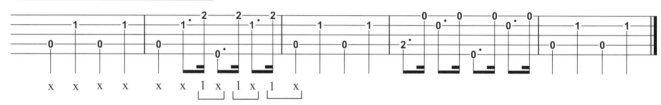

INTRODUCTION

In the latter example I have included brackets below the index-thumb finger combination positioned on the off-beats (for more information on the thumb-lead style please see my book, *Old Time String Band Banjo Styles*). Note here that Converse used the thumb consecutively for quarter notes in this arrangement; however, he more often than not used the index finger for those types of single note sequences.

Per standard clawhammer banjo style performance all notes on the first string are played only by the index finger and notes on the fifth string only by the thumb.

As many of these pieces were written in duple meter [2/4] I have taken the liberty to arrange them in Common time in order to minimize the use of repetitive 32nd note beaming which obscures the tab by making it appear too cumbersome and, at any rate, would probably intimidate many banjoists to the point of having them avoid learning these wonderful tunes altogether. The revised tab makes it easier to read in that it is visually similar to contemporary clawhammer banjo tab. Here is a comparison:

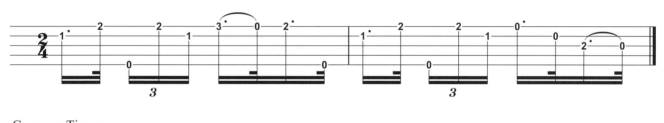

Common Time:

Let's look at a few comments that Converse provides. First, he says that the banjo is played in two different ways, the *Banjo* and *Guitar* styles of execution [down picking and parlor guitar finger styles respectively]; further, that "the 'Banjo' style is the most effective in giving expression to the peculiar quality and characteristics of *true Banjo music.*" Also,

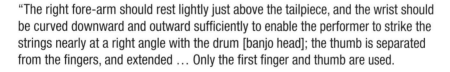

"The right fore-arm should rest lightly just above the tailpiece, and the wrist should be curved downward and outward sufficiently to enable the performer to strike the strings nearly at a right angle with the drum [banjo head]; the thumb is separated from the fingers, and extended … Only the first finger and thumb are used.

" … strike, with the first [index] finger, the string required, at the same time placing the thumb, *in anticipation*, on the string that is to produce the following tone; then, while raising the hand, vibrate, with the thumb, the string upon which it was placed, accompanying the action with a slight turning – outward and upward – of the hand in restoring it to its original position.

"**The act of striking resembles the movement of a hammer**, and should be clearly defined. The hand should be steadily controlled, and *short in its reaction time from the string*, that the movement may be repeated quickly when required."

INTRODUCTION

Preparing the thumb "in anticipation" is crucial with the index finger having to often strike notes on the unfamiliar upbeat.

Only two tunings are used for these pieces: the basic C tuning [gCGBD] and the open G tuning [gDGBD]; a number of the songs are in minor keys.

The Combination Movement. Converse calls the use of the index finger-thumb pattern a "combination movement." He then provides a number of basic exercises exploring this right hand finger movement. The first series focuses on "drop thumb" technique:

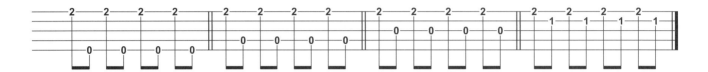

The second set focuses on the index finger moving from the first to the fourth string:

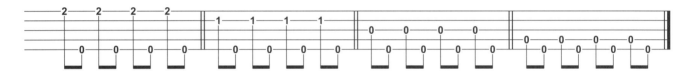

The final set focuses on notes played on the inside strings:

Unlike today's clawhammer arranging style Converse's is typical of 19th century banjo idiosyncrasies. In particular, you will notice the following:

- **Lots of dotted note figures**
- **Triplet combinations**
- **Grace note slurs**
- **Off-beat hammer-ons and pull-offs (2- and 3-note)**
- **Open string pulloffs**
- **Glide strokes (similar to today's Galax Lick)**

INTRODUCTION

The Half Combination. This note sequence consists of using the index finger to strike a single string while preparing the thumb on the fifth string; however, in this instance, after the index finger strikes its string, you simply remove the thumb from the fifth string without sounding it (shown in brackets in following example) because it has no note to play.

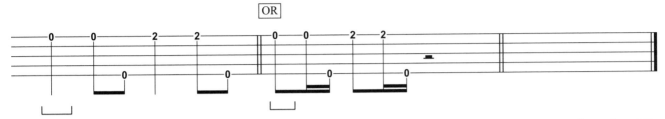

The Long Combination. This is similar to what today we call the Galax Lick. Converse describes it thus: " … sound the third string only (half combination) then, without raising the hand, push [glide] the finger across the remaining strings, and complete the combination by sounding the fifth string when recovering position." This technique can effectively be used in tunes in compound meter [6/8] as well. Here are several typical examples (the squiggly line represents the finger glide):

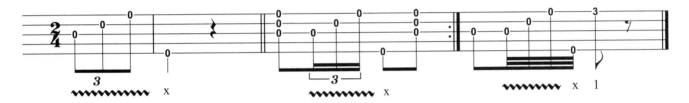

Sequential Triplet Figures. The use of triplet figures and back-to-back triplet figures are quite common in the 19th century banjo arrangements. The latter triplet is similar to a rolling arpeggio, thus you might call this combination sequence a rolling triplet; invariably, it beings with the Long Combination:

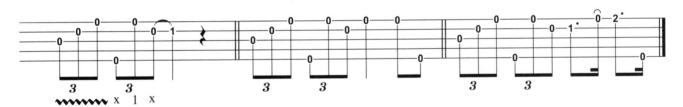

Syncopated Strokes. Many times Converse will use a syncopated stroke that is similar to today's usage of a eighth note-quarter note-eighth note sequence. I have chosen to use this rhythmic pattern in these arrangements vs. Converse's more intricate notation. Here is a comparison, first of what Converse used in 2/4 time, then how it looks when reduced to Common time, and then, finally, "smoothed out" with just eighth notes:

Original Converse   2/4 to Common Time   "Smoothed Out"

As you can see, the smoothed out version is much easier to read; just remember that it is a dotted figure note sequence and should be played thus.

INTRODUCTION

Melodic Style. The opening measures of the second section of *Grey Eagle Reel* show that Converse was adept in this style as well:

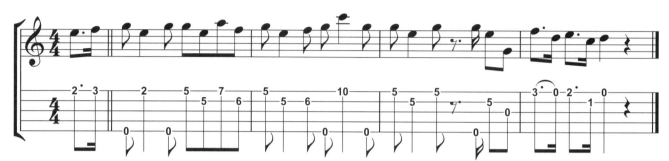

For more information on Converse's right hand arranging techniques please see my books, *More Minstrel Banjo: Frank Converse's Banjo Instructor* or *The Early Minstrel Banjo: Technique and Repertoire*. I will indicate in the tab any special right hand fingerings that Converse used for ease of interpretation; also included will be an appendix where I will provide some technical notes explaining particular potential trouble spots in certain songs, etc.

Alabama Walk-Around

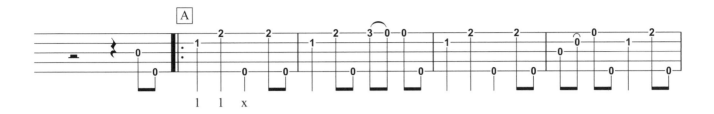

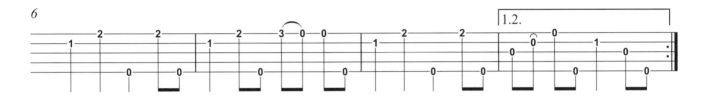

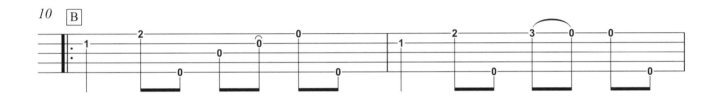

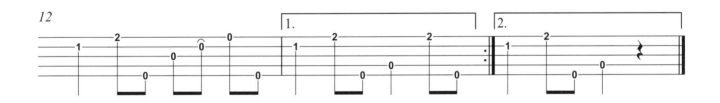

Arkansas Traveler

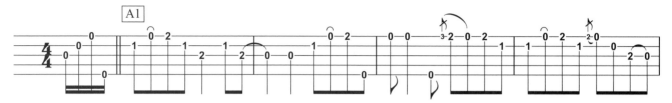

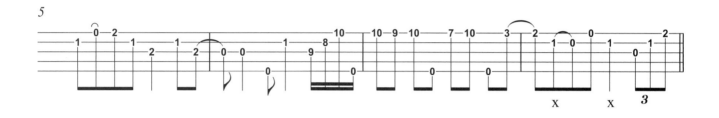

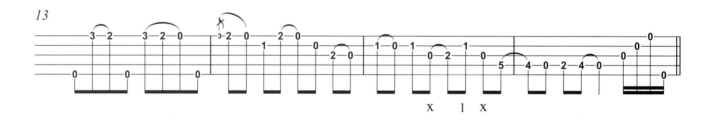

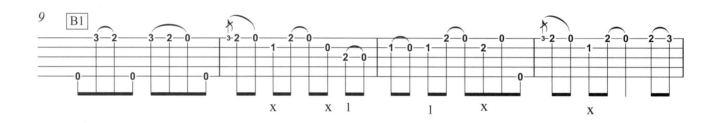

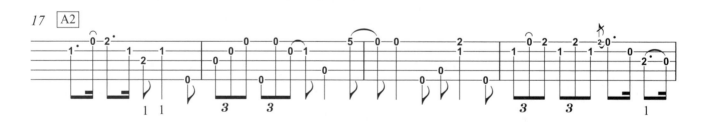

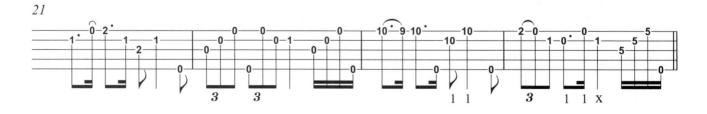

ARKANSAS TRAVELER

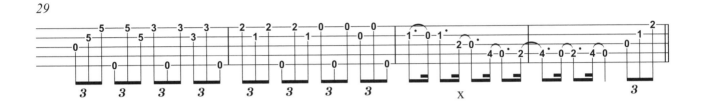

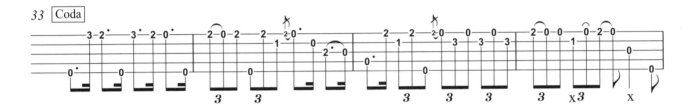

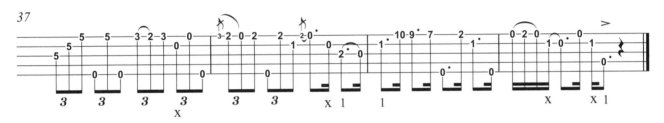

Anthony Street Reel

Open G Tuning

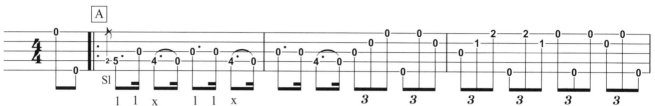

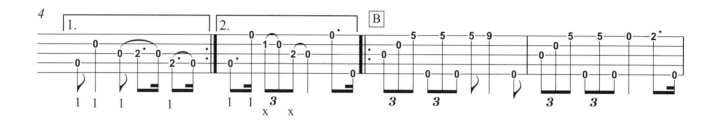

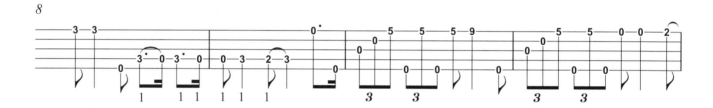

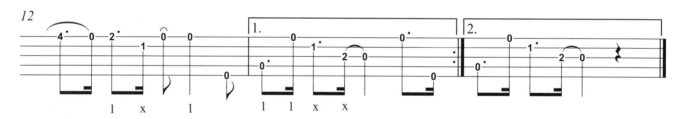

Boatman's Dance

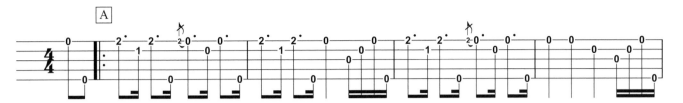

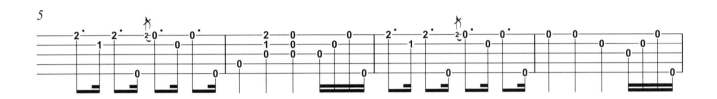

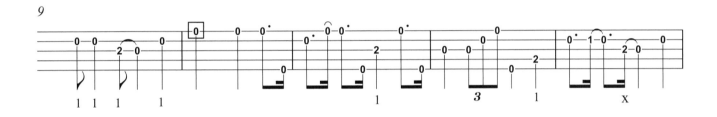

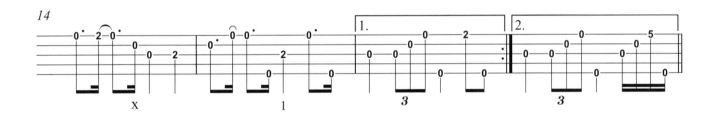

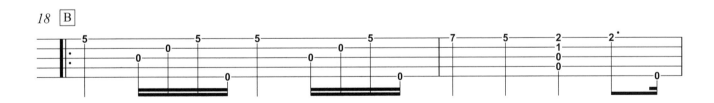

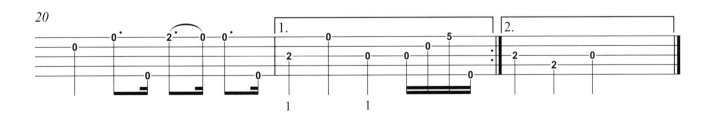

The Boxer's Reel

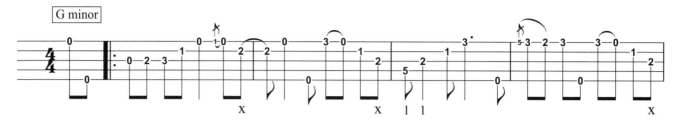

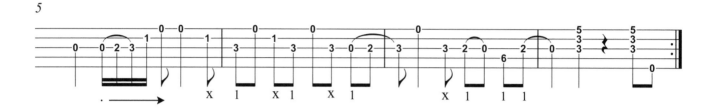

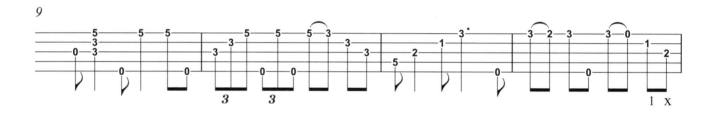

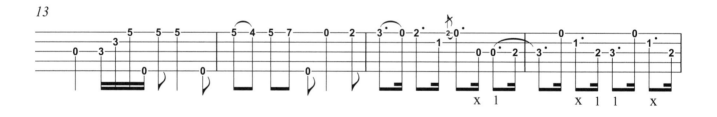

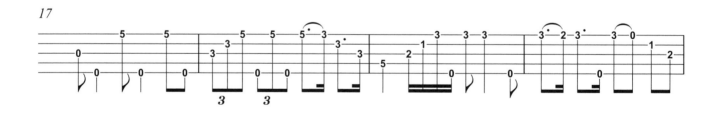

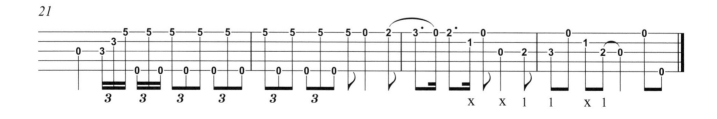

THE BOXER'S REEL

Presto: the windup

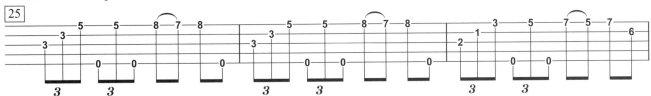

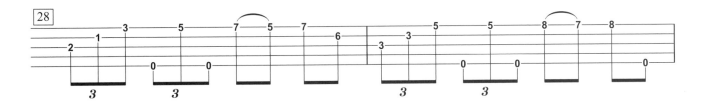

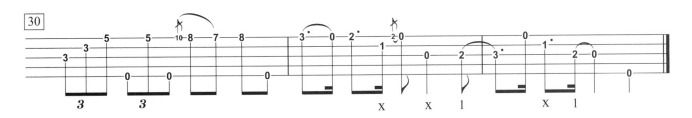

Brannigan's Reel

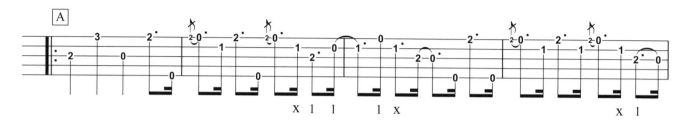

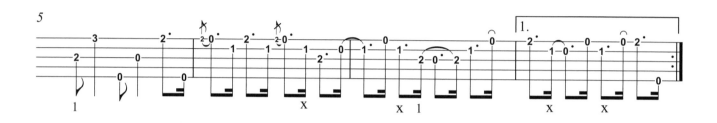

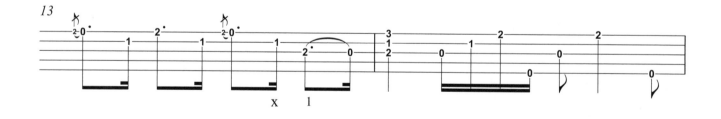

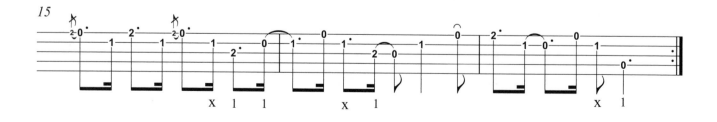

Camptown Race Track

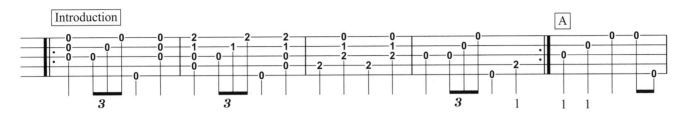

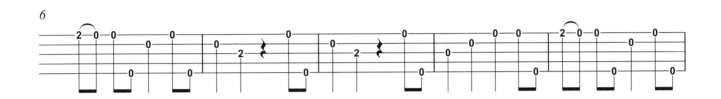

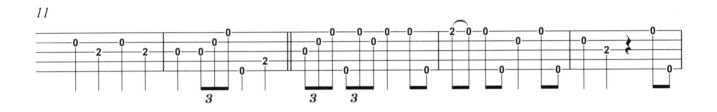

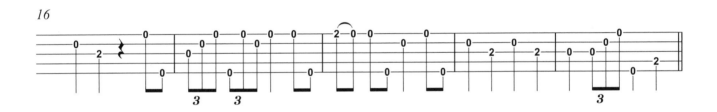

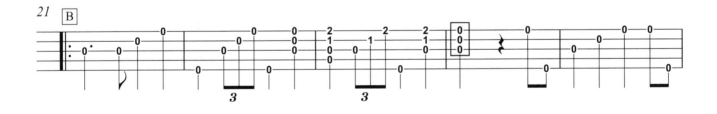

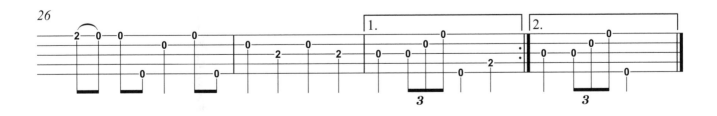

Cane Brake Reel

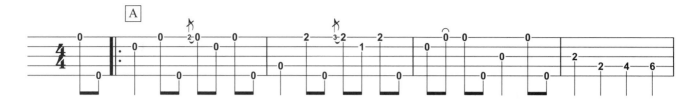

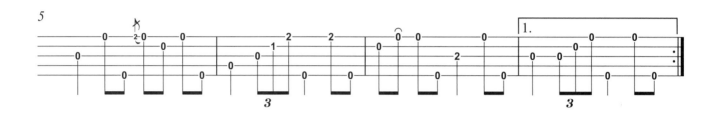

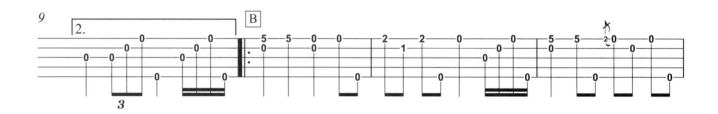

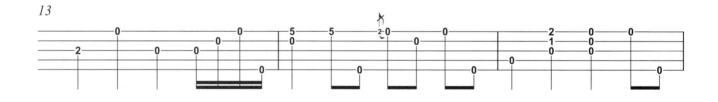

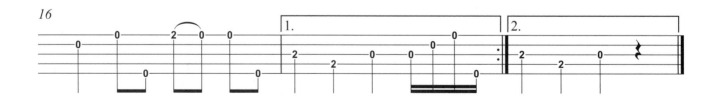

Carolina Reel

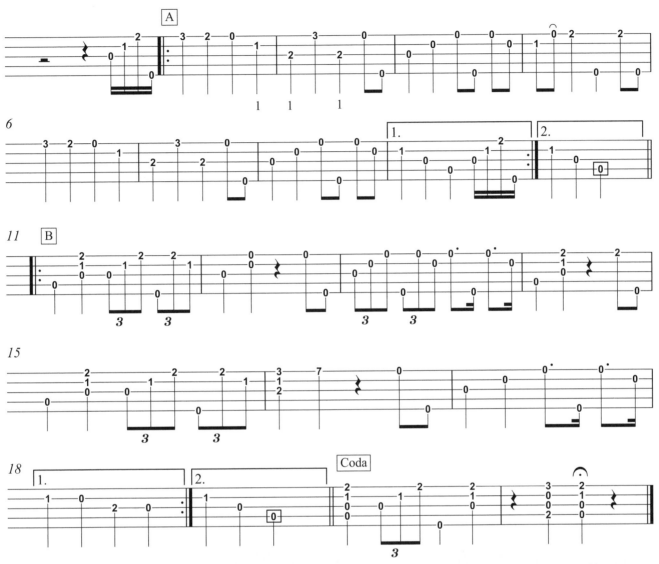

Choctaw Reel

Dark Horse Reel

Far South Reel Medley

FAR SOUTH REEL MEDLEY

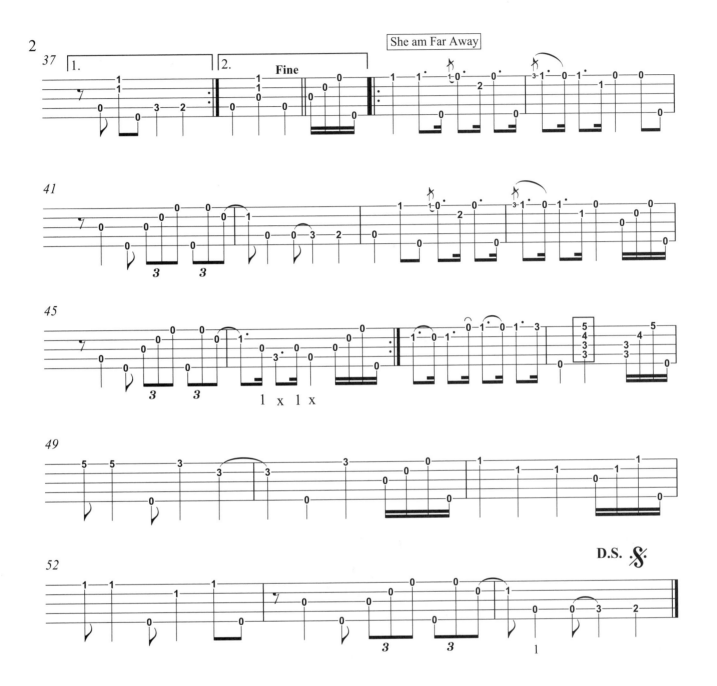

She am Far Away

Foster's Jig

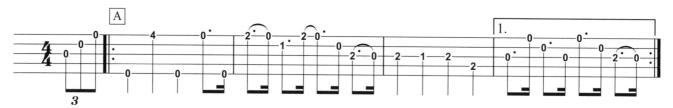

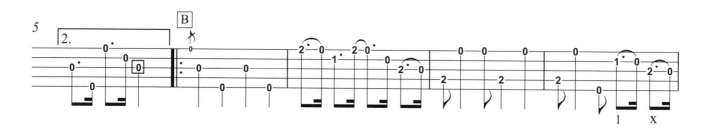

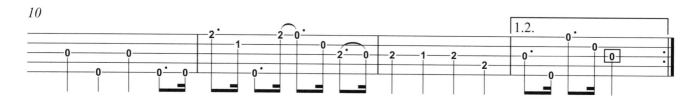

Frisky Reel

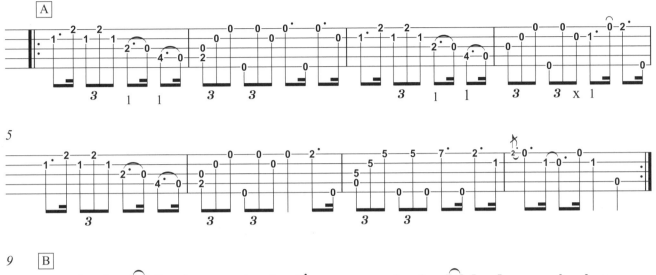

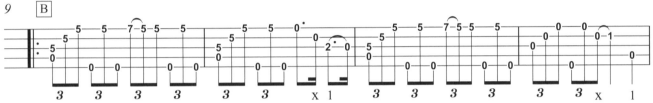

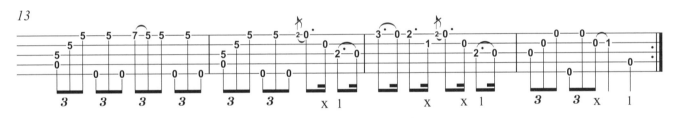

Hampton Medley

Open G Tuning

HAMPTON MEDLEY

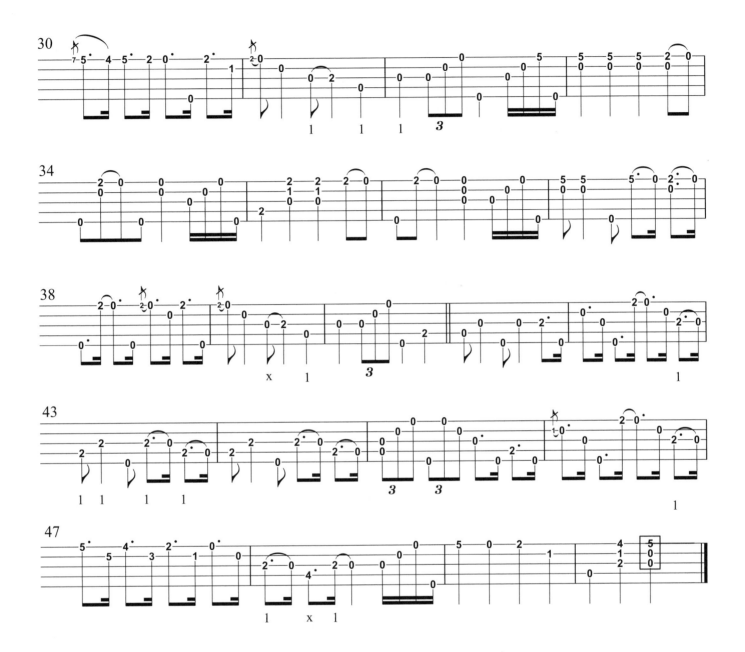

Grey Eagle Reel

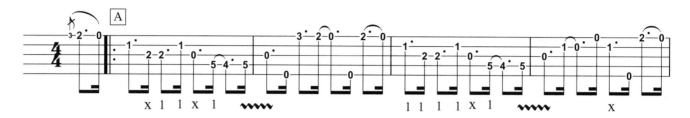

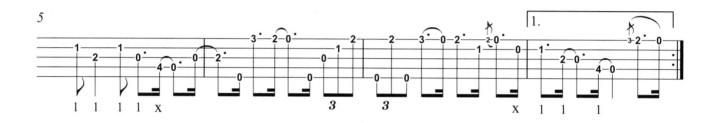

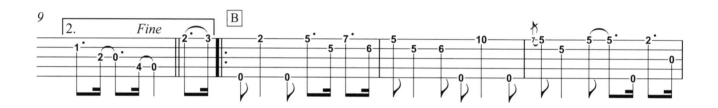

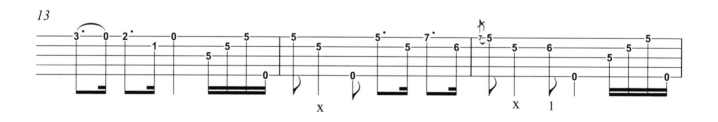

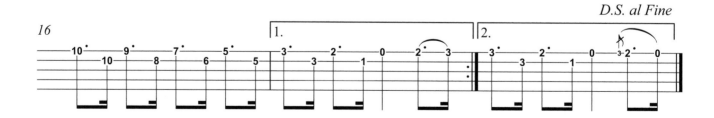

Irish Jig

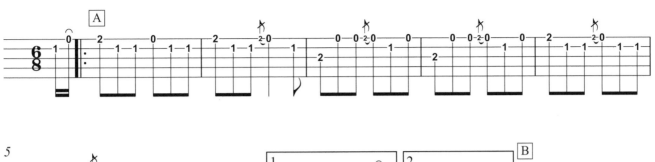

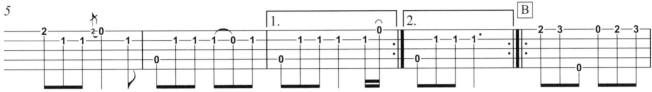

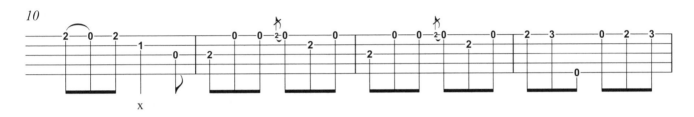

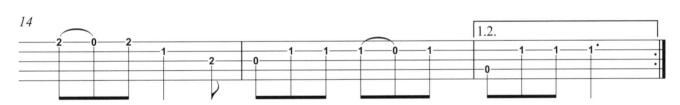

Jordan

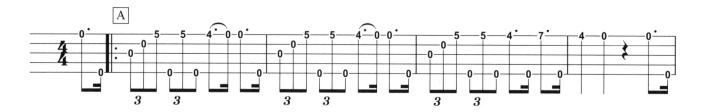

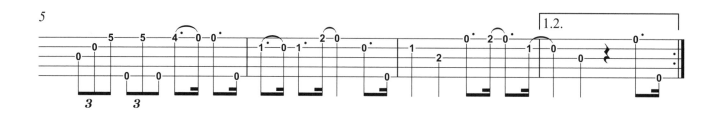

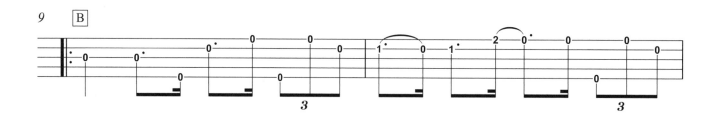

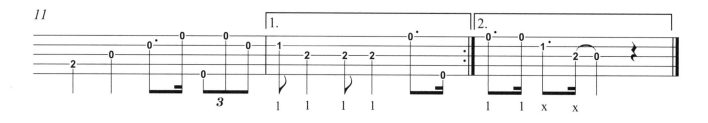

Jumbo Reel

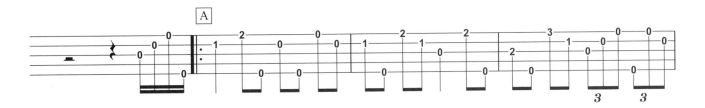

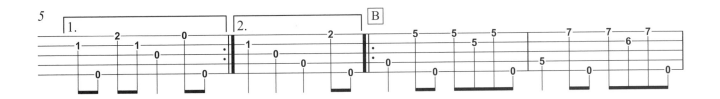

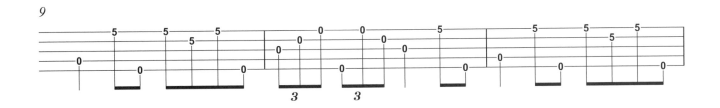

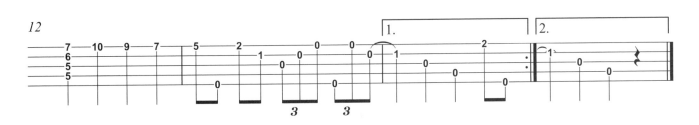

Leavitt's Jig

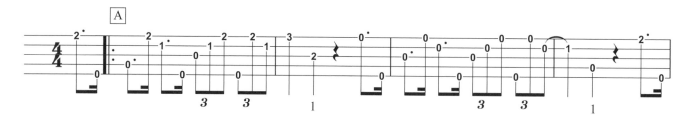

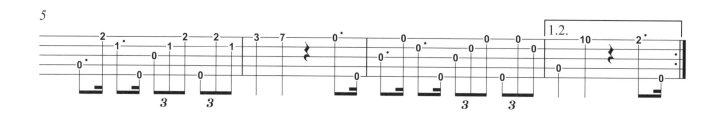

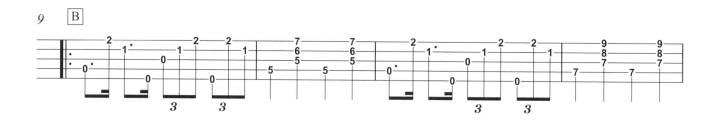

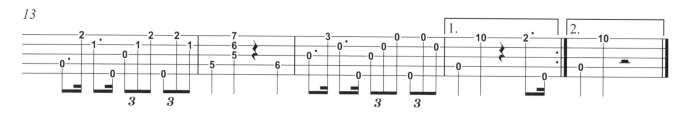

Lynchburg Reel

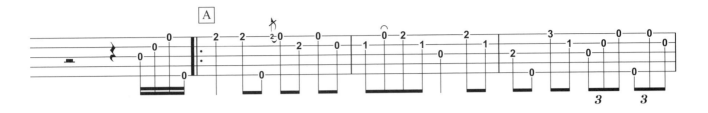

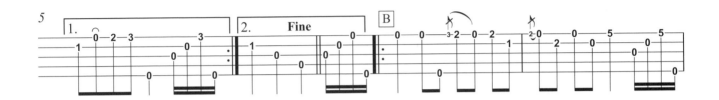

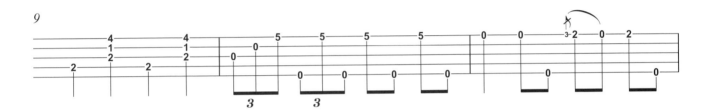

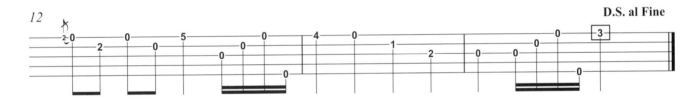

Mississippi Walk Around

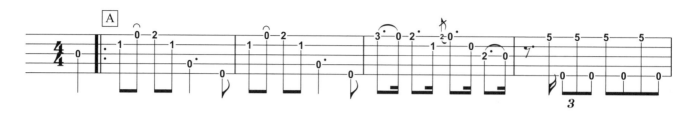

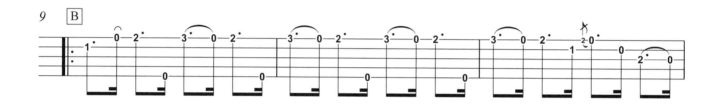

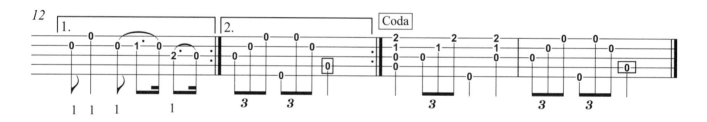

Modoc Reel

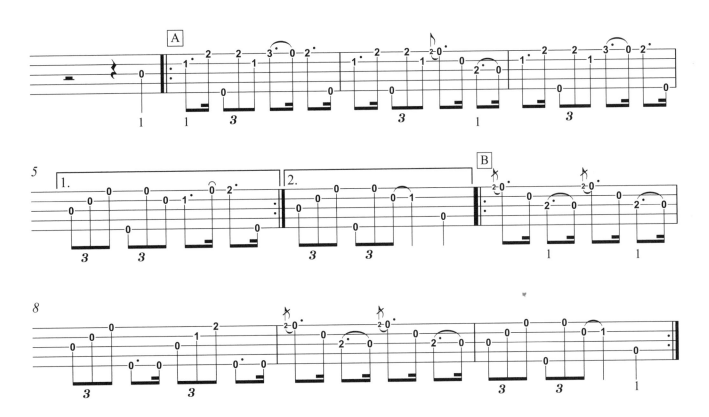

Narraganset Jig

NARRAGANSET JIG

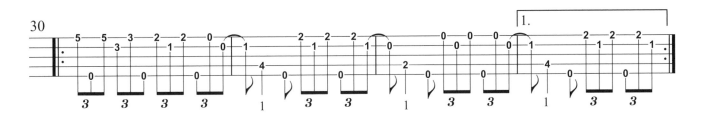

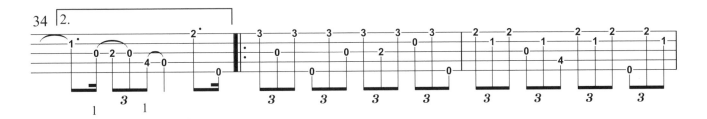

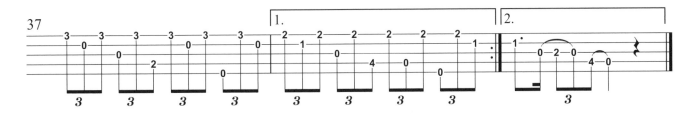

My Love is but a Lassie

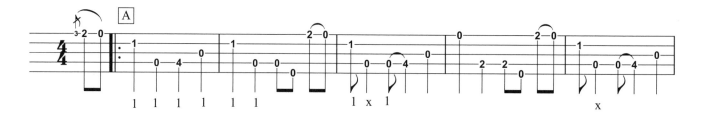

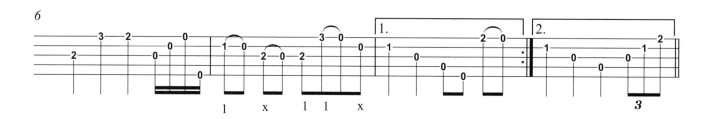

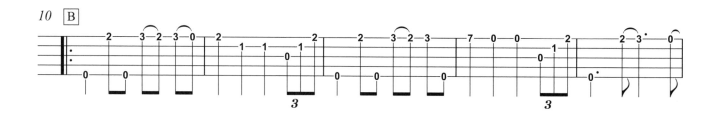

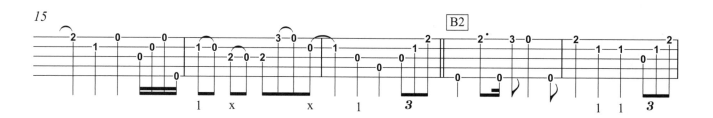

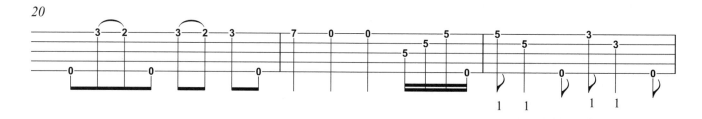

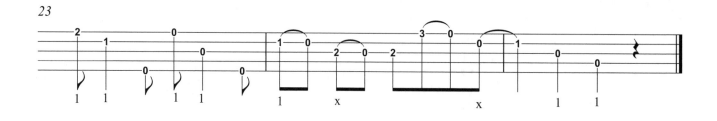

Old Plantation Reel

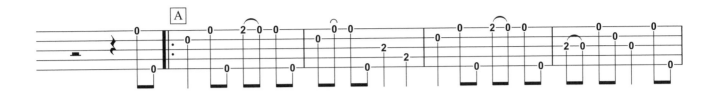

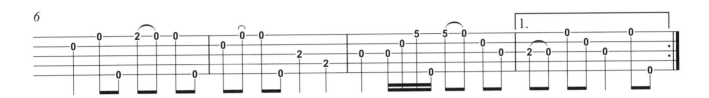

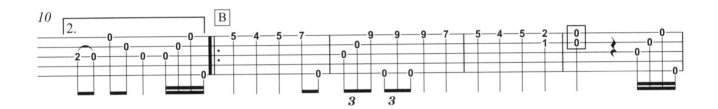

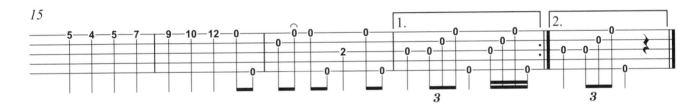

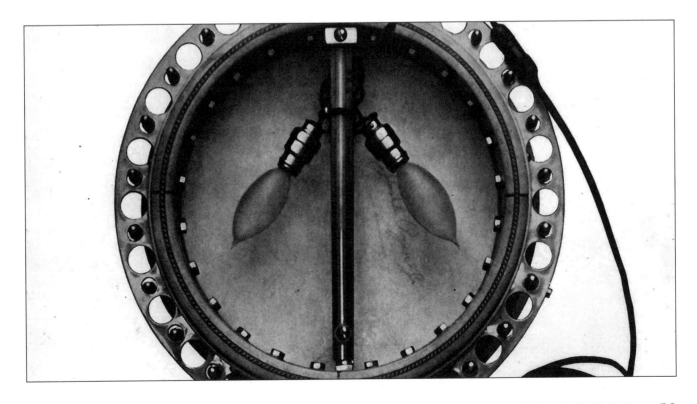

Old "Tuckapaw" Jig

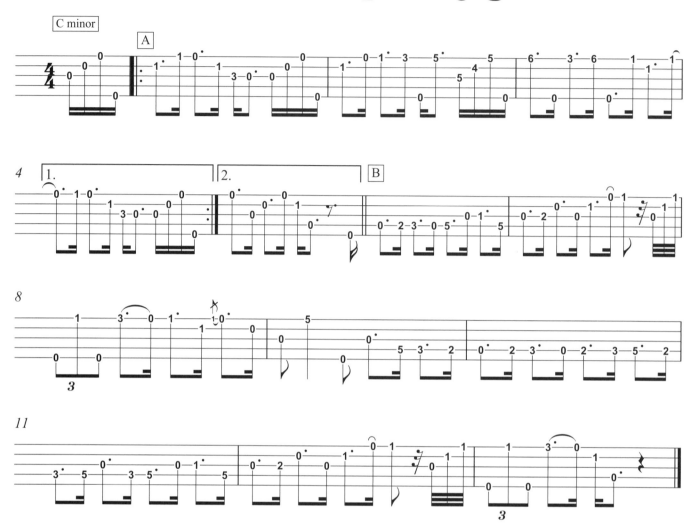

Old Virginny Dance

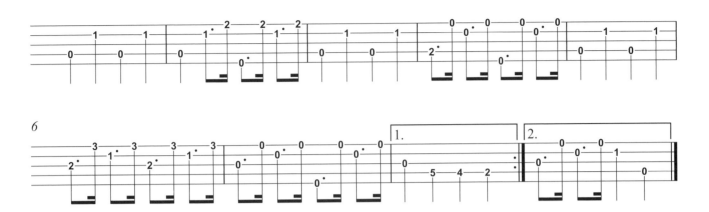

Old Zip Coon

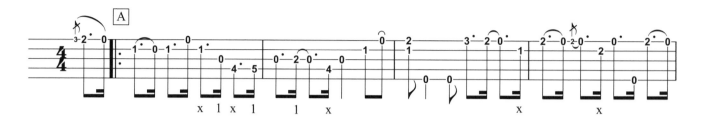

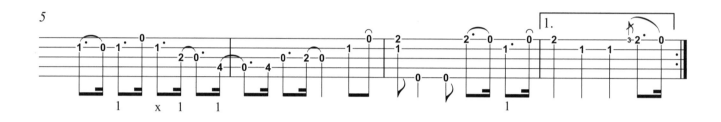

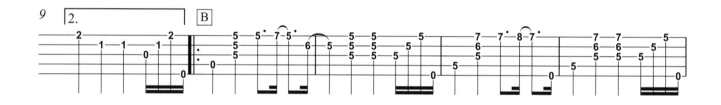

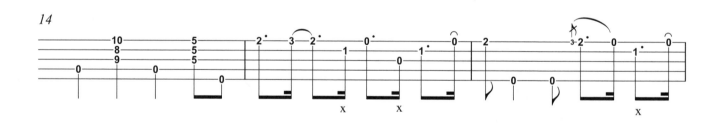

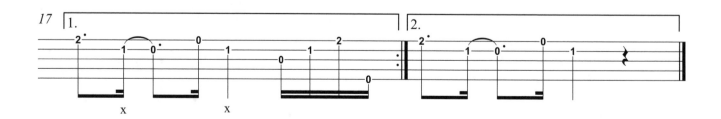

Philadelphia Jig

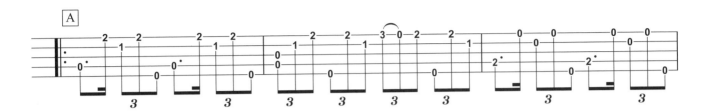

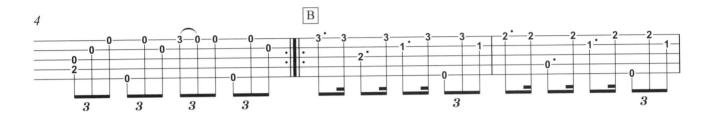

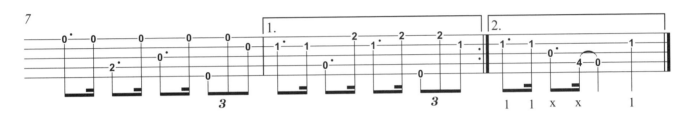

Rattlesnake Jig

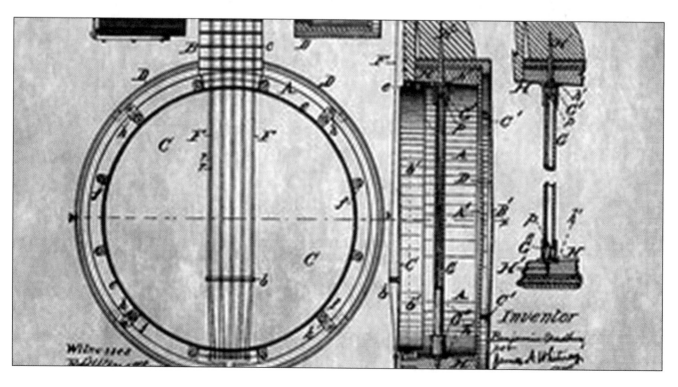

Short Stop Reel

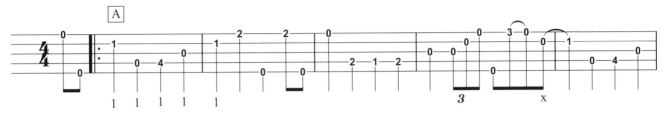

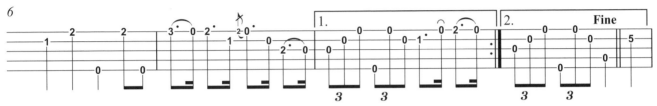

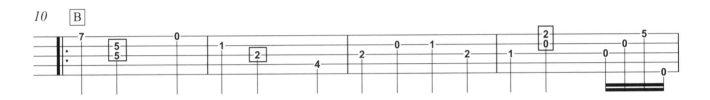

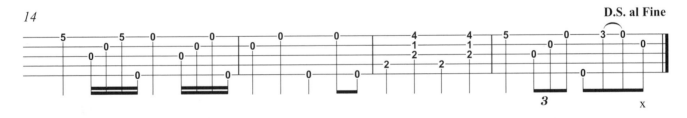

The Skidmore Guards

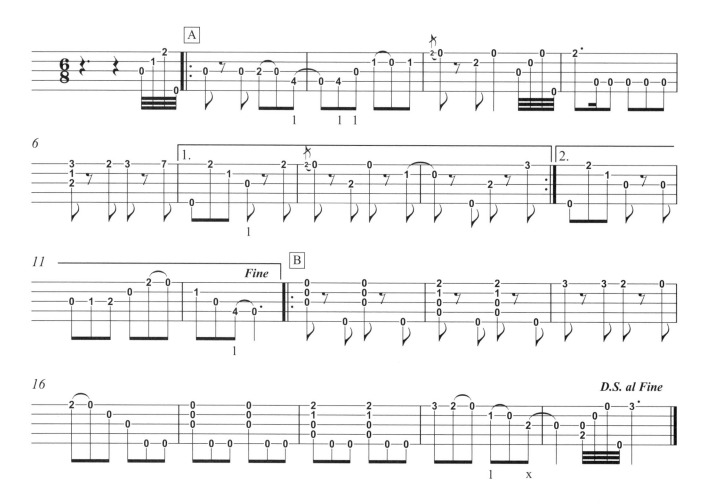

Sugar Cane Dance

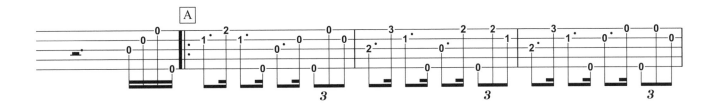

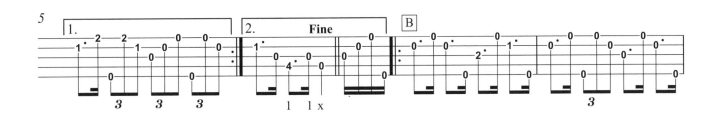

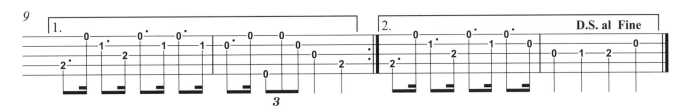

Sunrise Reel

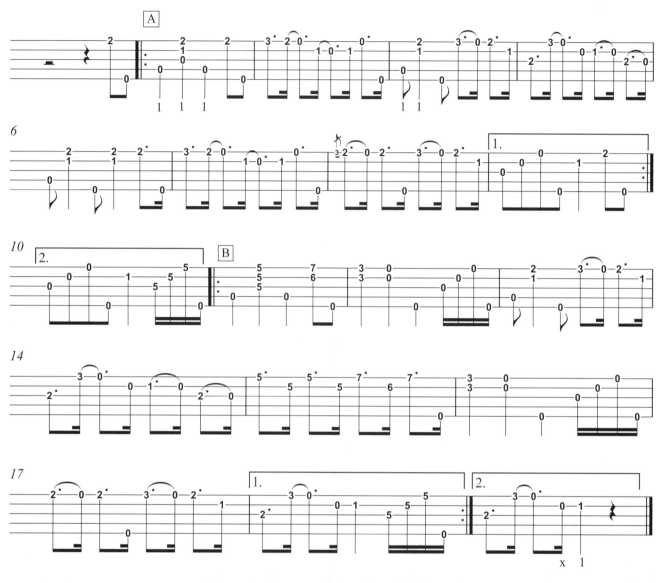

Texas Reel

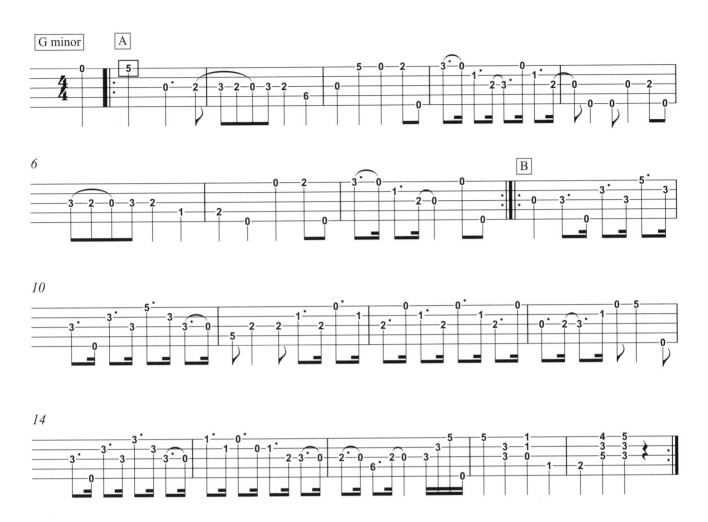

Walk into de Parlor

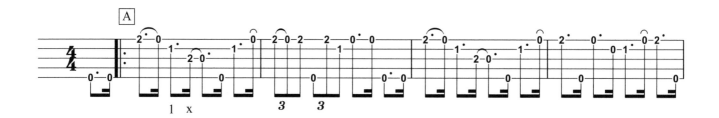

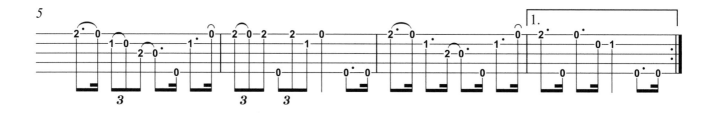

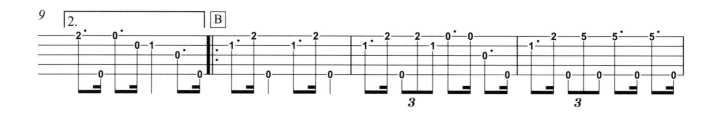

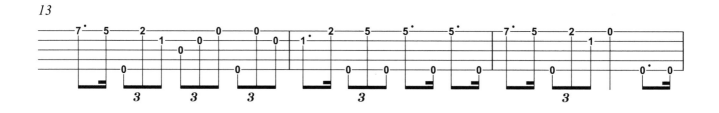

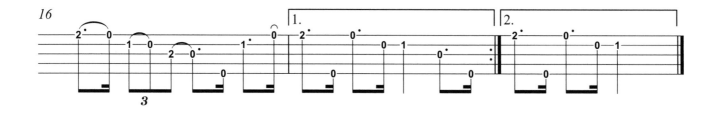

Water Street Reel

Open G tuning

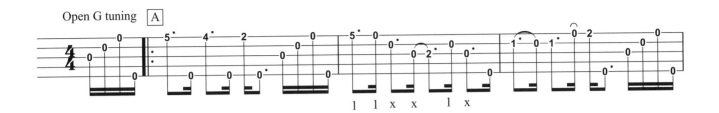

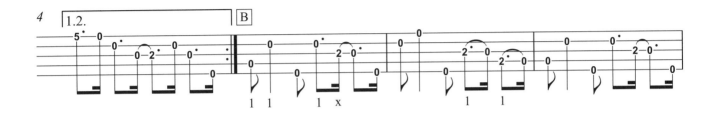

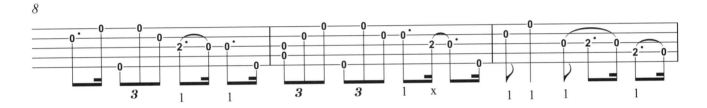

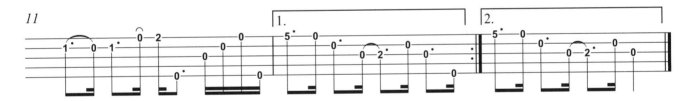

Wigwam Reel

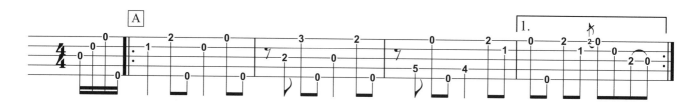

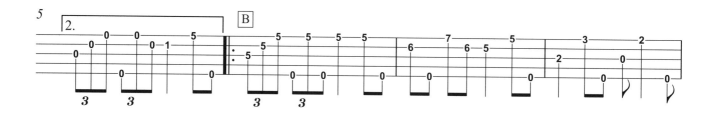

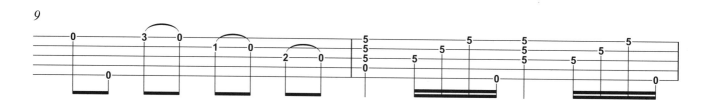

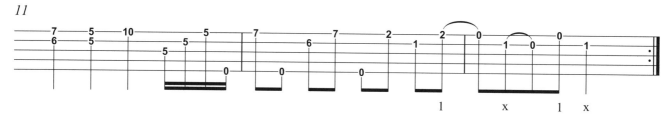

Appendix: Performance Notes

This is the order of the songs arranged in the banjo style as presented by Frank Converse in his 1887 method. I have provided detailed performance notes where I feel they might be useful. (Note: In some of the later songs I don't provide as many right hand fingerings because their usage was used in earlier tabs.)

OLD VIRGINNY DANCE
See the Introduction.

RATTLESNAKE JIG
On the last beat of measure 5 I use a thumb glide stroke from the fourth to the third string to lead back to the downbeat; similarly, I also do this at measure 12 when you go from the B section back to the A section.

This song presents the first use of a triplet figure, here at the beginning of the B section. Note the use of the index-thumb combination figure (shown below in brackets):

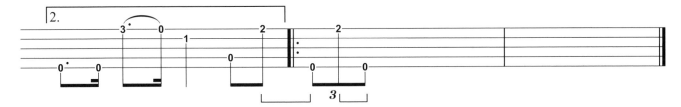

The B section features a call-and-response pattern in alternating measures.

The pickup to the second B section uses a triplet figure executed by use of the previously discussed long combination index finger glide; when you begin to play this figure make sure that you position your thumb on the fifth string so that it is ready to play.

In measure 12 we find the first use of a back-to-back triplet figure, a note sequence commonly used throughout these songs.

Note the B to C hammer on (slur) in the final measure of the B section; this slur is commonly used by Converse (but not always every time this phrase appears).

The final quarter note of the B section should be accented. This is accomplished by use of a **hammer stroke** in which the thumb crosses over the index finger as it would if you were holding a flat pick; the weight of the two fingers moving together creates a strong accent.

ALABAMA WALK AROUND
This song begins with a half-combination on the downbeat (see the Introduction). At measure 2 we encounter the first use of a **3 0 pull off** on the first string; this pull off graces this note sequence:

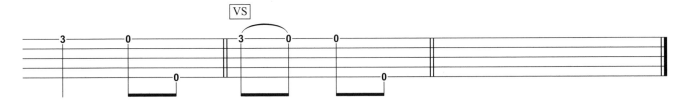

APPENDIX: PERFORMANCE NOTES

At measure 4 we find use of an open string pull off <u>on the second string</u> (instead of the more usually found first string usage in contemporary clawhammer banjo). This pull off connects a two beat note sequence, as shown below:

THE MODOC REEL

The downbeat of measure 1 shows another commonly used triplet combination:

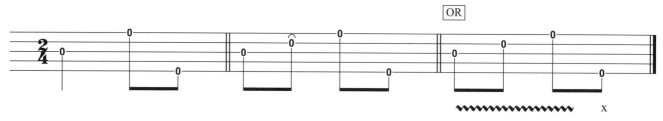

On beat three of measure 2 we encounter our first grace note which has been prepared by the previous note on the first string. I suggest that you initially play the phrase without the grace note, then, when comfortable, include it.

On beat three of measure 5 we find another open string pull off, this time part of a C chord. The best way to play this is to lift the index finger as you do the pull off, then reset the C chord fingering when you play the E note on beat four.

At measure 8 we find another commonly used note sequence begun by the long combination (similar to the southern Appalachian clawhammer Galax Lick figure):

In the final measure of the B section we once again encounter the B to C hammer on slur followed by a hammer stroke on the final note (as, for instance, used in *Rattlesnake Jig*).

CAMPTOWN RACE TRACK

This arrangement is pretty straight forward using all of the techniques previously introduced. The 3-note chords are played by using the aforementioned hammer stroke. Note the pull off usage at measure 6, similar to what I discussed under *Alabama Walk Around*.

At measures 13 and 17 note the use of back-to-back triplet figures.

APPENDIX: PERFORMANCE NOTES

SUGAR CANE DANCE

The pickup notes for this song are notated in 16th notes, i.e., one quarter note beat. Be sure to also practice them as two sets of eighth notes (two beats), as both are commonly used by Converse.

Note the right hand fingering for the second ending of the A section:

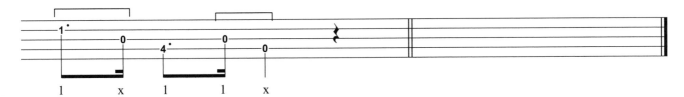

Also note that the last note of the second ending of the B section is an open second string (B), not C, as it leads back to the downbeat of Section A.

CAROLINA REEL

At the Measure 5 in Section A we once again find a first string open string pull off in a C chord.

Note the position shift needed at measure 16 from the third to the seventh fret (I suggest using a *portamento* slide using the little finger).

SUNRISE REEL

In Measure 2 we encounter pull offs positioned on off beats, while measure 3 sees the use of the syncopated rhythm (as discussed in the Introduction).

A 3-string bar is used in Measure 11; however, when the phrase is repeated at measure 15 only a 2-string double stop is required.

Note that in the final measure Converse again doesn't use the B to C slur to end the song, as he frequently does.

OLD PLANTATION REEL

Measure 2 features use of the standard clawhammer open string pull off on the first string. On beat three in Measure 7 I use the middle finger to stop the A on the third string and then use the index finger to stop the D on the fourth string (I prefer using this finger combination when this note sequence appears).

On the downbeat of Section B I use the middle finger on the fifth fret; after playing the fourth fret with the index finger I then shift the index finger up to the fifth fret. In Measure 13 I again use the middle finger to stop the fifth fret note; this is useful as I then use it to shift down to the C chord at the end of that measure.

In Measure 16 I use the index finger to stop the note at the ninth fret to set up the left hand fingering for that measure.

APPENDIX: PERFORMANCE NOTES

LYNCHBURG REEL

The last note in Measure 7 is a C on the second string; however, when that phrase is repeated in Measure 11 the score instead notates use of the E note on the first string. I prefer to repeat the phrase identically, i.e., using the C note.

In Measure 9 Converse uses a D7 chord; however, I usually play a D chord instead:

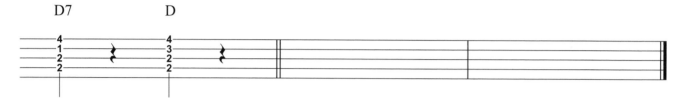

IRISH JIG

This is the first of two songs in 6/8 meter in the banjo style found in Converse's method (the other is *The Skidmore Guards*). The right hand fingering alternates every two measures in the A section, index-thumb-thumb, then all index. At Measure 10 make sure that you use the combination stroke beginning on the third eighth note.

In Section B I switch fingers for the ornament played at Measure 12: ring finger for the grace note, then the second finger for the C# note on the second string (which means taking it off of the A note on the downbeat of that measure).

JUMBO REEL

In Measure 7 I use a two-string barre, switch to a full barre in the following measure, then back to the two-string barre in Measure 9. After the full barre on the downbeat at Measure 12 I shift to the seventh position to play the descending notes ending that measure. At Measure 13 I once again use the second finger for the fifth fret note then shift down with it to the C chord.

LEAVITT'S JIG

Note the position shift at the beginning of Measure 6; as the third fret is stopped by the little finger I simply shift it up to stop the note at the seventh fret (a sliding *portamento* movement works nicely). A similar type of sudden jump occurs at both the end of the A and B sections.

In Measures 10 and 14 a sudden shift is called for from first to fifth position. What works best for me is to release the finger pressure on the C chord, then shift; the ringing of the open fifth string masks this shift without incident.

On the third beat of Measure 14 (a quarter note rest) I release the F chord, and then use the third finger to stop the sixth fret on the fourth string.

APPENDIX: PERFORMANCE NOTES

CANE BRAKE REEL

In the fourth measure I once again use the second-first finger overlap (see *Old Plantation Reel*), then shift the index finger up to the fourth fret allowing the ring finger to stop the following note at the sixth fret.

Measure 15 calls for use of the hammer stroke for the chords on beats two and three.

MISSISSIPPI WALK AROUND

Measures 4 and 8 call for no note to be played on either downbeat; simply tap your foot to keep the rhythm going.

Measure 12 calls for a two-note pull off (used fairly frequently by Converse).

The last note of the song, in the Coda, is the low C on the open fourth string, <u>not</u> the expected C on the second string.

PHILADELPHIA JIG

On the downbeats in Measures 2 and 4 a double note is used to begin the long combination; similarly, in the same measures, a pull off is used on the third triplet figure.

Note the repeated thumb usage for the final ending of the song.

FOSTER'S JIG

For the most part Converse uses mostly thumb strokes in this arrangement, even where he would normally use index-thumb; in contrast, at the end of the song at Measures 12-13, he primarily uses index finger strokes.

Note the grace note which begins Section B. To execute this note pair I suggest that you simultaneously move the index and thumb on the first and third strings to make these two notes sound as seamless as possible.

BOATMAN'S DANCE

On the pickup note to Section A I suggest using a dotted note figure. Regarding the open string pull off found at Measure 15 I suggest using the middle finger to execute this slur because the second finger is stopping the A note at the end of the previous measure.

WIGWAM REEL

In Section A note the syncopations in Measure 2 and 3 caused by an eighth note rest on those two downbeats. At the second ending I slide the second finger up to the fifth fret on the first string, then barre the fifth fret as I play the open fifth string.

At Measure 12 Converse uses a melodic style passage. Also make note the right hand fingering for the last two measures of Section B.

APPENDIX: PERFORMANCE NOTES

GREY EAGLE REEL

Note the grace note on the pickup note pair creating a two-note slur. Otherwise, observe all of the right hand fingerings indicated throughout Section A.

As mentioned in the Introduction, make note of the Melodic Style of arranging in Section B.

FRISKY REEL

No comments.

THE SKIDMORE GUARDS (QUICK STEP)

Observe the rhythm of the pickup notes in this song, as it is in 6/8 time. The four 16th notes are equivalent to two beats in 6/8 time, so don't play four eighth notes by mistake.

WALK INTO DE PARLOR

Note the two pickup notes, as both notes on the open fifth string.

Compare the notes in Measure 5 to those in Measure 7: the only difference is the pull off on the triplet figure.

In Measures 12 and 14 I use the second finger to shift from the second to the fifth fret on the first string leaving the fourth finger free to play the note at the seventh fret.

OLD ZIP COON [AKA TURKEY IN THE STRAW]

The song begins with a grace note on the pickup note figure, creating a two-note slur.

Watch out for the barring required in Measures 10 through 14.

JORDAN

In the opening measures I use the second finger for the fifth fret note leaving the index finger free for the fret below and the little finger for the note at the seventh fret on beat four in Measure 3.

This arrangement also uses a melodic style fragment from beat 3 in Measure 3 to beat 3 in Measure 4.

WATER STREET REEL [OPEN G TUNING]

This was the first song in the banjo style of arranging where Converse used a Scotch Hop rhythm: it is simply the reverse of what he usually uses, i.e., this time the dotted note is the second note of the pair.

In Measures 2 and 4 you may wish to use a **5 0 pull off** instead of playing each note separately by the index finger. This results in a different right hand fingering:

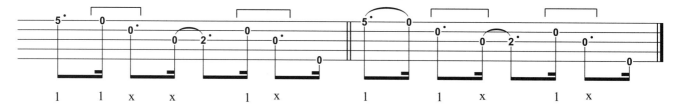

APPENDIX: PERFORMANCE NOTES

MISCELLANEOUS PIECES (AS FOUND UNDER CONVERSE'S "DIVISION NO. 4")

The final songs in this collection call upon all of the techniques you have been using: syncopation rests on downbeats, barre chords, quick position shifts and rapid finger changes. I will point the most intricate areas and how I finger those note sequences.

ANTHONY STREET REEL

This song opens up with a slide. I use the middle finger to slide up to the fifth fret leaving the index finger free to play the note at the fourth fret on the same string.

At Measures 6 and 10 I stop the fifth fret note with the index finger so that the little finger can stop the note at the ninth fret.

In Measure 8 I play the third fret on the first string with my ring finger, the middle finger then stopping the lower octave note on the third fret of the fourth string, and then the index finger for the note one fret lower in Measure 9.

In Measure 12 the open string pull off on the first string at beat four is best played by using the middle finger.

MY LOVE IS BUT A LASSIE

The dotted notes found in Measure 14 are actually doubly dotted for a prolonged delay; however, my music software program wouldn't allow me to write out this subdivision in banjo tab.

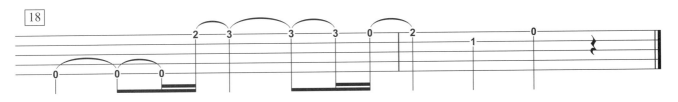

Watch out for the descending syncopated note sequence beginning at Measure 22.

BRANNIGAN'S REEL

On the fourth note in Measure 10 I use the little finger, and then shift it up to the fifth fret, then up to the tenth fret on the following downbeat for the C chord inversion. Also, make note the open string pull off on the first string required on the last note in the penultimate measure.

SHORT STOP REEL

Note the use of the low C note on the fourth string at the second ending. This allows you to shift up to the fifth position and finger the A minor chord at the beginning of Section B.

Once again I play a D chord instead of a D7 chord at Measure 16.

APPENDIX: PERFORMANCE NOTES

NARRAGANSETT JIG

The Scotch Hop rhythm is used in Measures 3, 22 and 27. This song also features lots of rests positioned on downbeats; in particular, note those in Measure 18!

At Measure 9 I use the middle finger to shift from the second fret to the fifth fret which allows me to then use the little finger for the note at the seventh fret.

On the last note in Measure 23 the score calls for the use of an E note on the fourth string, fourth fret, which is the fifth scale tone of the A minor scale. However, I feel that is it better to instead play the A note on the third string, second fret, as this prepares for it usage on the following downbeat following the quick grace note slur.

At Measure 30 I use the <u>little</u> <u>finger</u> to stop the two notes on the first and second strings as the fifth fret. I then can use my index finger to barre the first two strings at the third fret.

At Measure 35 Converse incorporates a moving melodic line within a series of triplet figures. Very clever!

FAR SOUTH REEL MEDLEY [C MINOR]

This is another song which features lots of rests on downbeats.

At Measure 5 I use the third finger to shift down from the fifth fret down to the third fret on the first string.

At Measure 21 I use the index finger to stop the note at the fifth fret, then jump up to the 10th fret where I use the middle finger, then shift back down with the middle finger to the fifth fret allowing the index finger to stop the following note at the third fret.

The last note of Measure 25 marks a modulation to the key of E flat. At Measure 28 I use my third finger to shift from the fifth to the 10th fret, then down again, this time to the third fret; similarly, I also shift it down from the fifth to the third fret at Measure 32.

HAMPTON MEDLEY CHARACTERISTIC [OPEN G TUNING]

At beat three in both Measures 3 and 4 release the C chord fingering as the chord changes at that point to G, so harmonically it will sound better. At Measure 17 I use the second finger on the second fret then shift it up to the fifth fret, then down again.

On the last beat of Measure 46 I suggest shifting to second position, i.e., stopping the note on the second fret of the third string with the index finger thus making it easier to finger the following double stop at the fifth fret.

Finally, once again, I use the D chord fingering for the penultimate chord in the last measure.

APPENDIX: PERFORMANCE NOTES

CHOCTAW REEL

Note that Converse uses the index finger instead of the expected thumb in Measures 1 and 5 on the next to last note. Watch out for the quick shift at Measure 10 (I usually shift on the last open fifth string of the triplet figure); it is probably easiest to use the C chord fingering for the double stop on beat 3 in Measures 10 and 14.

THE BOXER'S REEL [G MINOR]

Note in Measure 5 that Converse notates the use of an <u>unprepared</u> thumb stroke on the last sixteenth note of beat 2! At measure 14 you need to change left hand fingers on the fifth fret from the ring finger (as used in the preceding measure) <u>to</u> the middle finger (this is done similarly for the note sequence in measures 25 and 26). Make note that two different triplet rhythms are used in Measure 21-22.

In Measures 25 and 26 I use the middle finger to shift from the fifth fret to the eighth fret, then down again. Similarly, in Measures 27 and 28 over the F chord, a different left hand fingering is called for during the shift. In this case, as you play the open fifth string on beat 2 shift to the fifth position so that the index finger is used for the note at the fifth fret on the first string (and the middle finger for the note at the sixth fret of the second string).

OLD "TUCKAPAW" JIG [C MINOR]

The Scotch Hop rhythm is used on the third beat in Measure 1 as well as on the final beat of the song. In Measure 2 I use the ring finger to shift from the third to the fifth fret while the open fifth string is played on beat three; the little finger is thus free to play the sixth fret for the note sequence following the C minor chord.

For the pull off on the last note of Measure 3 I use the middle finger to stop the first fret on the first string to smoothly execute the pull off (I also use this technique for the grace note pull off on beat four in Measure 8).

At Measure 7 I use the ring finger to execute the open string pull off on the first string.

Make sure that you work out a smooth left hand fingering for Measures 9 through 11!

*DARK HORSE REEL [C MINOR]

This is a very intricate song to play, so please be patient!! Converse indicates use of the index finger <u>instead</u> of the thumb on the second note of the first measure. I use the middle finger to execute the pull off at the end of the first measure (instead of the index finger) which then allows me time to easily prepare for the following barre figure.

The first sixteenth note triplet that appears in the first ending of Section A is rhythmically part of the <u>previous</u> eighth note; the following eight note triplet is then the pickup figure for a return to the downbeat in measure one.

APPENDIX: PERFORMANCE NOTES

Be prepared for the position shift at the beginning of Measure 6; as they are both quarter notes you have plenty of time. Since my little finger is shorter than the norm I execute a shift after the C minor chord on the second beat and use the ring finger to play the pull off at the twelfth fret; I then return to the middle finger for the following pull off figure which is then part of the C minor chord barre fingering.

The broken chord note sequence at Measures 8 through 10 works fine if you use a three string barre at the 8th fret.

TEXAS REEL [G MINOR]

Measure 1 begins in second position. At the end of Measure 2 I usually use my middle finger to stop the note at the sixth fret on the fourth string (a small shift is required to do so), although you could also use your little finger to stop that note. I then use my middle finger to stop the following note at the fifth fret on the first string, then, when playing the next open string note on the first string, I shift back to first position.

I use my index finger to shift from the first to second fret on the fourth string across the bar line connecting Measure 6 to Measure 7; similarly, I also do this at Measures 17 and 18 to end the song.

At Measure 10 I use my middle finger to play the pull off on beat four. Watch out for the index-thumb combination movements in Measures 11 and 12.

ARKANSAS TRAVELER

At Measure 29 I use the little finger to bar the notes at the fifth fret, then the index finger for the barre at the third fret (this technique was discussed earlier). This series of triplets is simply an index-thumb alternation between the first and fifth strings, then the first and second strings; practice it as a series of eighth notes, then as triplets.

Notice the Scotch Hop which ends the arrangement (and with use of the hammer stroke to emphatically end the song).

More Great Banjo Books from Centerstream...

BEGINNING CLAWHAMMER BANJO

 DVD

by Ken Perlman

Ken Perlman is one of the most celebrated clawhammer banjo stylists performing today. In this new DVD, he teaches how to play this exciting style, with ample close-ups and clear explanations of techniques such as: hand positions, chords, tunings, brush-thumb, single-string strokes, hammer-ons, pull-offs and slides. Songs include: Boatsman • Cripple Creek • Pretty Polly. Includes a transcription booklet. 60 minutes.

00000330 DVD $19.95

INTERMEDIATE CLAWHAMMER BANJO

DVD

by Ken Perlman

Picking up where *Beginning Clawhammer Banjo* leaves off, this DVD begins with a review of brush thumbing and the single-string stroke, then moves into specialized techniques such as: drop- and double-thumbing, single-string brush thumb, chords in double "C" tuning, and more. Tunes include: Country Waltz • Green Willis • Little Billie Wilson • Magpie • The Meeting of the Waters • Old Joe Clark • and more! Includes a transcription booklet. 60 minutes.

00000331 DVD $19.95

CLAWHAMMER STYLE BANJO

TAB DVD

A Complete Guide for Beginning and Advanced Banjo Players

by Ken Perlman

This handbook covers basic right & left-hand positions, simple chords, and fundamental clawhammer techniques: the brush, the "bumm-titty" strum, pull-offs, and slides. There is also instruction on more complicated picking, double thumbing, quick slides, fretted pull-offs, harmonics, improvisation, and more. Includes over 40 fun-to-play banjo tunes.

00000118 Book Only $19.95
00000334 DVD $39.95

THE EARLY MINSTREL BANJO

TAB

by Joe Weidlich

Featuring more than 65 classic songs, this interesting book teaches how to play the minstrel banjo like players who were part of various popular troupes in 1865. The book includes: a short history of the banjo, including the origins of the minstrel show; info on the construction of minstrel banjos, chapters on each of the seven major banjo methods published through the end of the Civil War; songs from each method in banjo tablature, many available for the first time; info on how to arrange songs for the minstrel banjo; a reference list of contemporary gut and nylon string gauges approximating historical banjo string tensions in common usage during the antebellum period (for those Civil War re-enactors who wish to achieve that old-time "minstrel banjo" sound); an extensive cross-reference list of minstrel banjo song titles found in the major antebellum banjo methods; and more. (266 pages)

00000325...$29.95

MELODIC CLAWHAMMER BANJO

A Comprehensive Guide to Modern Clawhammer Banjo

by Ken Perlman

Ken Perlman, today's foremost player of the style, brings you this comprehensive guide to the melodic clawhammer. Over 50 tunes in clear tablature. Learn to play authentic versions of Appalachian fiddle tunes, string band tunes, New England hornpipes, Irish jigs, Scottish reels, and more. Includes arrangements by many important contemporary players, and chapters on basic and advanced techniques. Also features over 70 musical illustrations, plus historical notes, and period photos.

00000412 Book/CD Pack $19.95

MINSTREL BANJO – BRIGGS' BANJO INSTRUCTOR

TAB

by Joseph Weidlich

The Banjo Instructor by Tom Briggs, published in 1855, was the first complete method for banjo. It contained "many choice plantation melodies," "a rare collection of quaint old dances," and the "elementary principles of music." This edition is a reprinting of the original Briggs' *Banjo Instructor*, made up-to-date with modern explanations, tablature, and performance notes. It teaches how to hold the banjo, movements, chords, slurs and more, and includes 68 banjo solo songs that Briggs presumably learned directly from slaves.

00000221...$12.95

MORE MINSTREL BANJO

TAB

by Joseph Weidlich

This is the second book in a 3-part series of intabulations of music for the minstrel (Civil War-era) banjo. Adapted from Frank Converse's *Banjo Instructor, Without a Master* (published in New York in 1865), this book contains a choice collection of banjo solos, jigs, songs, reels, walk arounds, and more, progressively arranged and plainly explained, enabling players to become proficient banjoists. Thorough measure-by-measure explanations are provided for each of the songs, all of which are part of the traditional minstrel repertoire.

00000258...$12.95

WITH MY BANJO ON MY KNEE

The Minstrel Songs of Stephen Foster
arr. for banjo by Daniel Partner
Historical notes by Edwin J. Sims

Here are some of the first and most popular songs ever written for banjo. Fascinating historical notes accompany this collection, describing the meaning of the songs, their place in history, the significance of the musicians who first performed them, and Foster himself, America's first professional songwriter. The complete original lyrics of each song and an extensive bibliography are included. The CD contains recordings of each arrangement performed on solo minstrel banjo.

00001179 Book/CD Pack $19.95

P.O. Box 17878 - Anaheim Hills, CA 92817
(714) 779-9390   www.centerstream-usa.com

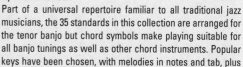